Solo Pieces for the BEGINNING DESCANT/SOPRANO RECORDER

By Costel Puscoiu

Online PDF www.melbay.com/98171EB

I0806901

MEL BAY®

Visit us on the Web at www.melbay.com — E-mail us at email@melbay.com

Contents

		Piano	Soprano Recorder
Spring	Costel Puscoiu	3	3
Madrigal	Michael Praetorius	4	3
Hungarian Dance (No.1)	Johannes Brahms	5	3
Air (from Sonata No.9)	Wolfgang Amadeus Mozart	6	4
Easy	Costel Puscoiu	8	4
March	Costel Puscoiu	9	6
Greensleeves	Old English Song	10	6
Gavotte	Arcangelo Corelli	12	7
Melody	Costel Puscoiu	13	7
Papageno's Carillon	Wolfgang Amadeus Mozart	14	7
Tiribomba	Italian Folk Song	15	9
The Beginner	Costel Puscoiu	16	9
Melody	Nicolai Rimsky-Korsakov	17	9
Moscow Nights	Russian Folk Song	18	10
Children's Dance	Costel Puscoiu	19	10
Krakowiak	Polish Folk Song	20	10
Pavane	Gabriel Fauré	21	11
Adagio (from Clarinet Concerto)	Wolfgang Amadeus Mozart	22	11
Prelude (Op.28, No.7)	Frédéric Chopin	24	13
Two Pigeons	Argentinian Folk Song	25	13
Morning (from "Peer Gynt")	Edvard Grieg	26	13
Album – leaf (from "Lyric Pieces")	Edvard Grieg	28	14
Slavonic Dance (Op.46, No.2)	Antonin Dvořák	30	15
Romance (Op.50)	Ludwig van Beethoven	31	15

Spring

Costel Puscoiu
(1951)

Madrigal

Michael Praetorius
(1571 - 1621)

Hungarian Dance

(No. 1)

Johannes Brahms
(1833 - 1897)

Air
(from Sonata No. 9)

Wolfgang Amadeus Mozart
(1756 - 1791)

p
p

Easy

Costel Puscoiu
(1951)

Allegretto grazioso

March

Costel Puscoiu
(1951)

Greensleeves

Old English Song

mf
mf
D.C. al Fine
D.C. al Fine

Gavotte

Arcangelo Corelli
(1653 - 1713)

Allegretto

Melody

Costel Puscoiu
(1951)

Papageno's Carillon

(from "The Magic Flute")

Wolfgang Amadeus Mozart

(1756 - 1791)

Tiribomba

Italian Folk Song

The Beginner

Costel Puscoiu
(1951)

Melody
(from "Scheherazade")

Nicolai Rimsky-Korsakov
(1844 - 1908)

Allegretto

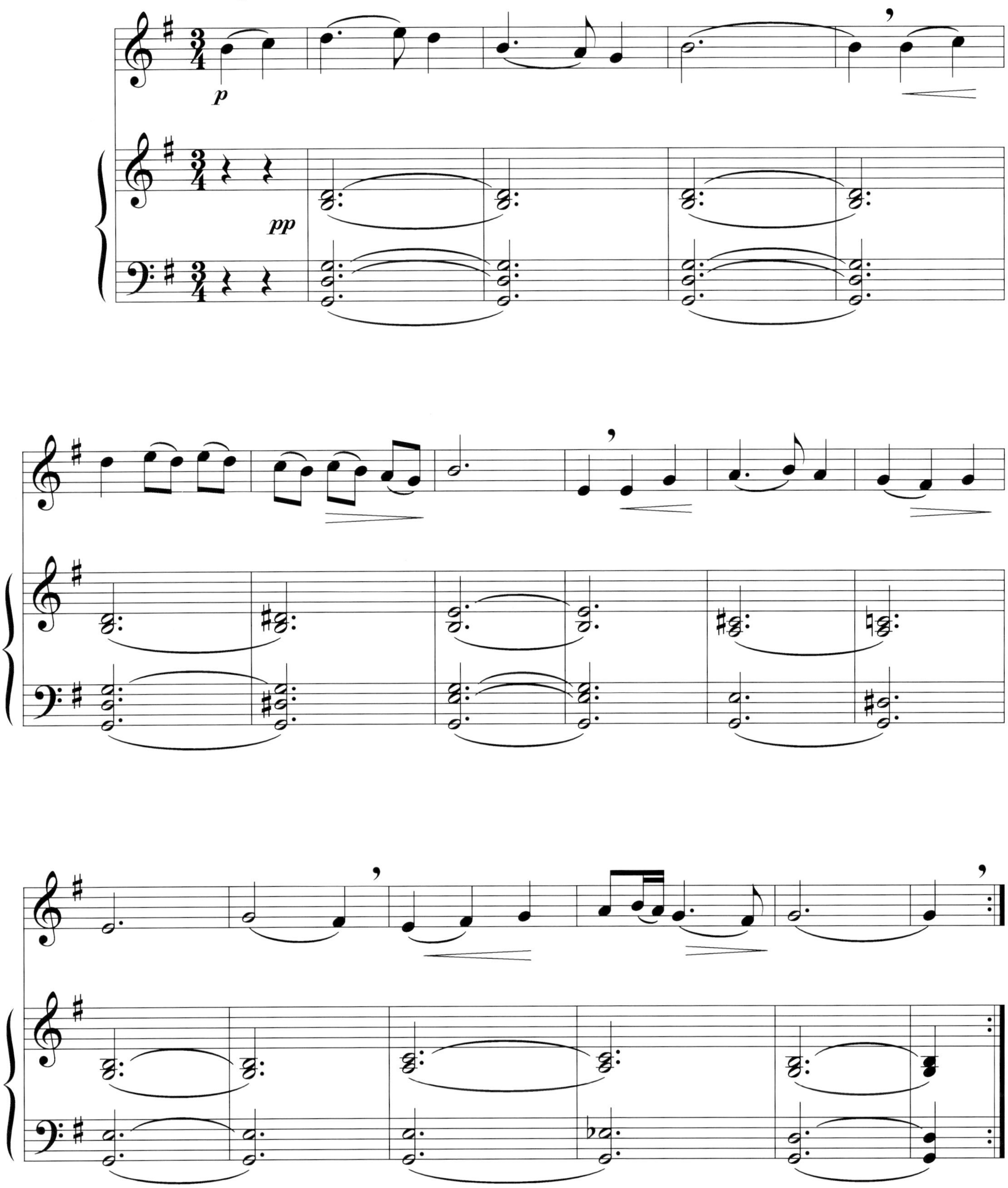

Moscow Nights

Russian Folk Song

Children's Dance

Costel Puscoiu
(1951)

Moderato

Krakowiak

Polish Folk Song

Pavane

Gabriel Fauré
(1845 - 1924)

Adagio
(from Clarinet Concerto)

Wolfgang Amadeus Mozart

(1756 - 1791)

Adagio

p
p
f
f

Prelude

(Op. 28, No. 7)

Frédéric Chopin
(1810 - 1849)

Two Pigeons

Argentinian Folk Song

Morning

(from "Peer Gynt")

Edvard Grieg
(1843 - 1907)

Allegretto pastorale

mf
mf
f
f
piu f
rit.
piu f
rit.

Album-leaf

(from "Lyric Pieces")

Edvard Grieg

(1843 - 1907)

dolce

Slavonic Dance

(Op. 46, No. 2)

Antonin Dvořák
(1841 - 1904)

Allegretto grazioso

Romance

(Op. 50)

Ludwig van Beethoven
(1770 - 1827)

Solo Pieces
for the
BEGINNING DESCANT/SOPRANO RECORDER

By Costel Puscoiu

Descant/Soprano Recorder

Visit us on the Web at www.melbay.com — E-mail us at email@melbay.com

Contents

Spring

Costel Puscoiu
(1951)

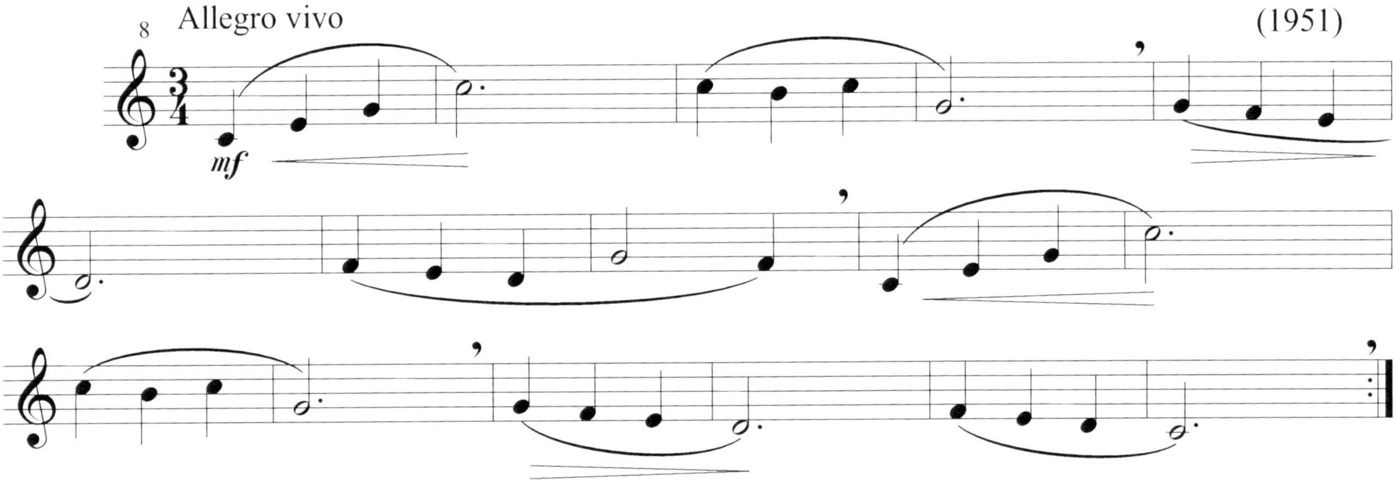

Madrigal

Michael Praetorius
(1571 - 1621)

Hungarian Dance

(No.1)

Johannes Brahms
(1833 - 1897)

Air
(from Sonata No. 9)

Wolfgang Amadeus Mozart
(1756 - 1791)

Andantino

Easy

Costel Puscoiu
(1951)

Allegretto grazioso

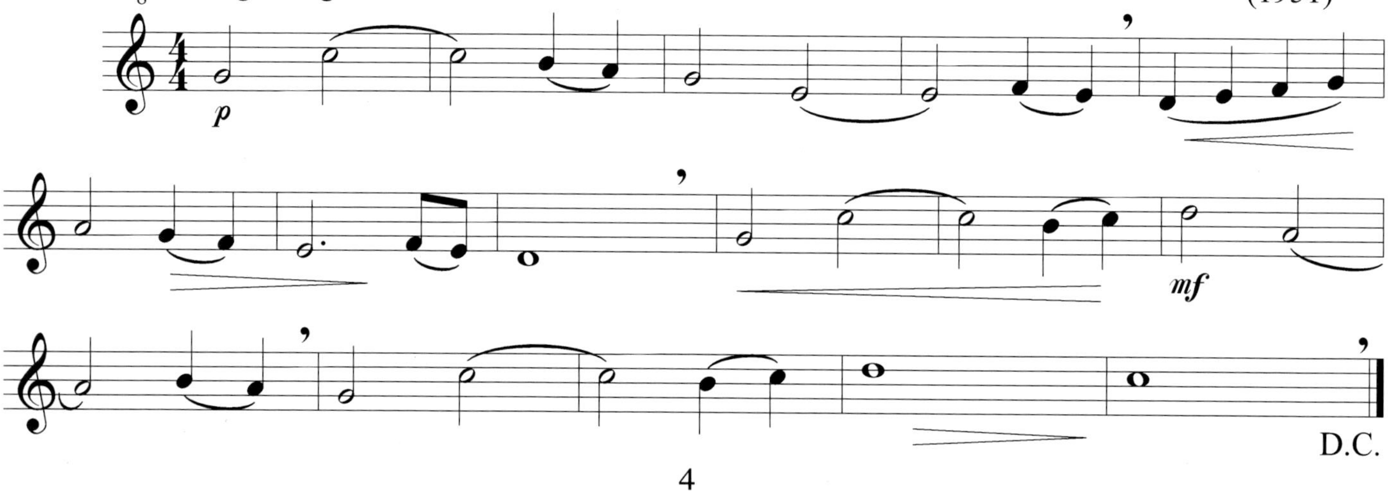

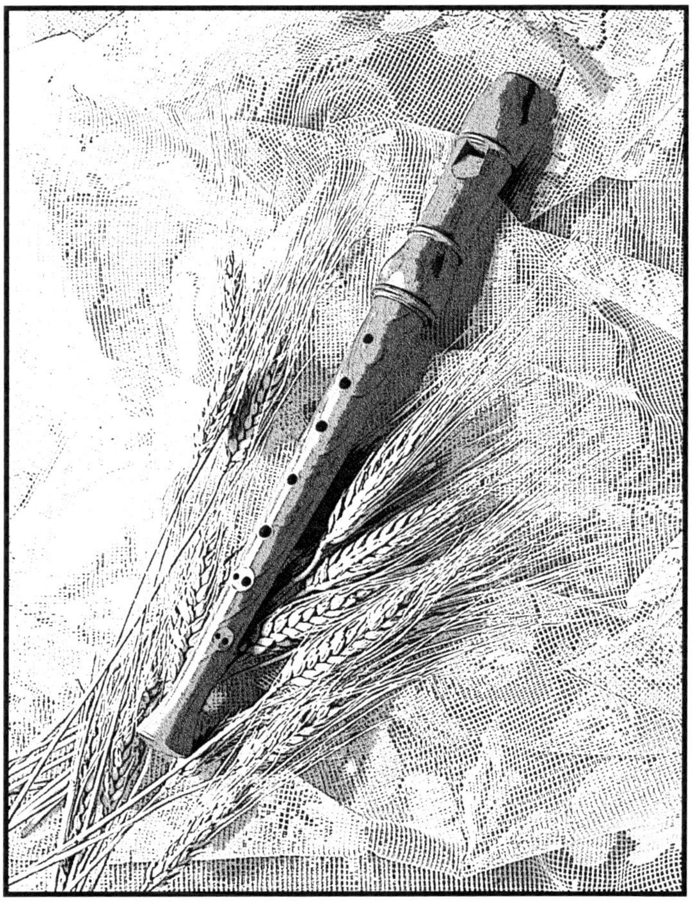

March

Costel Puscoiu
(1951)

Greensleeves

Old English Song

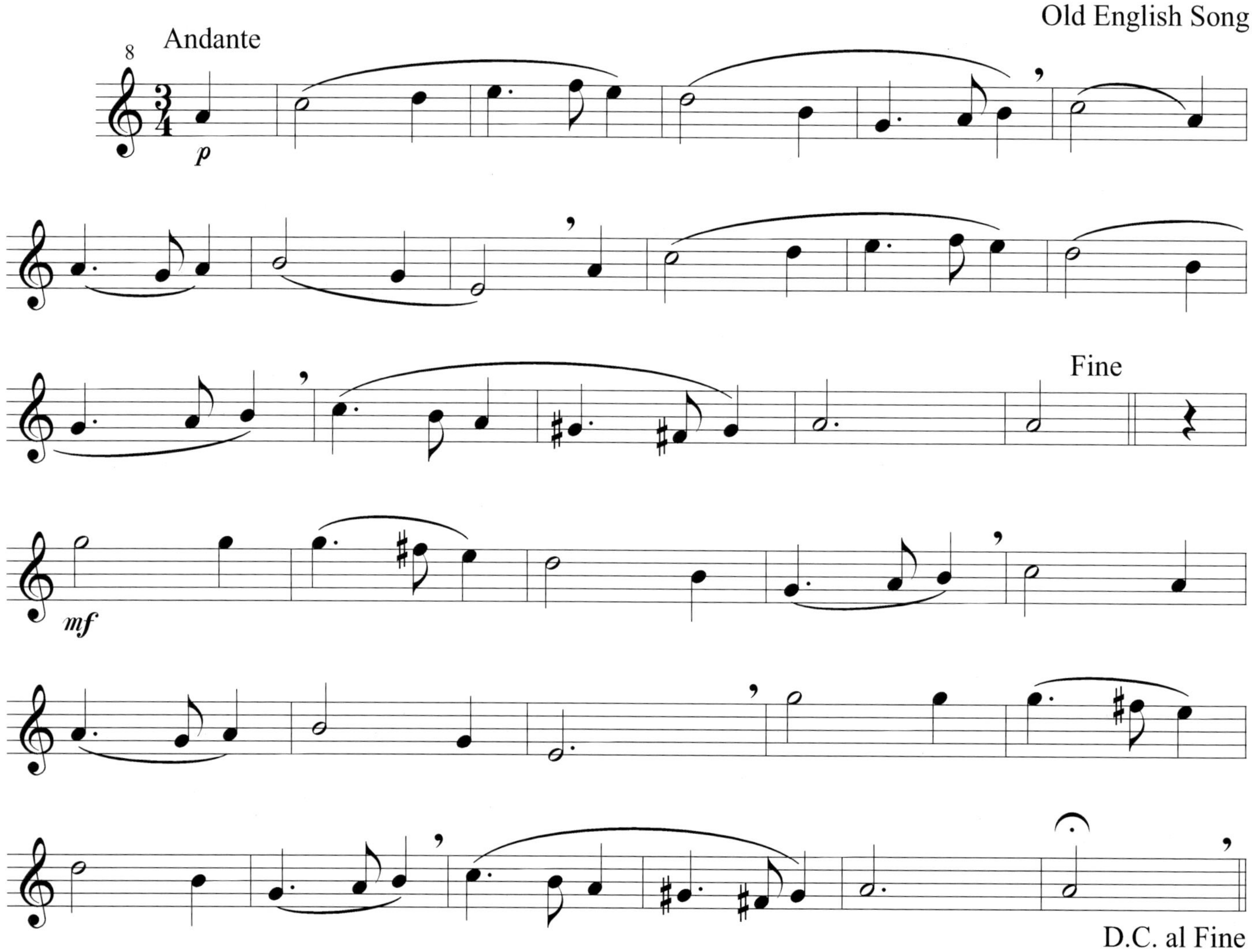

Gavotte

Arcangelo Corelli
(1653 - 1713)

Melody

Costel Puscoiu
(1951)

Papageno's Carillon

(from "The Magic Flute")

Wolfgang Amadeus Mozart
(1756 - 1791)

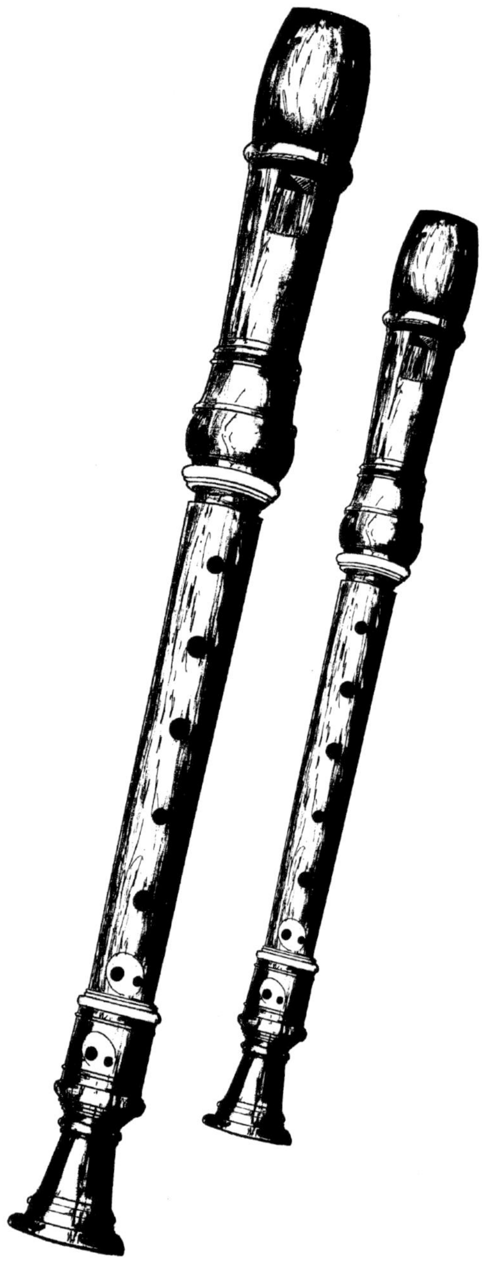

Tiribomba

Italian Folk Song

The Beginner

Costel Puscoiu
(1951)

Melody

Nicolai Rimsky-Korsakov
(1844 - 1908)

Moscow Nights

Russian Folk Song

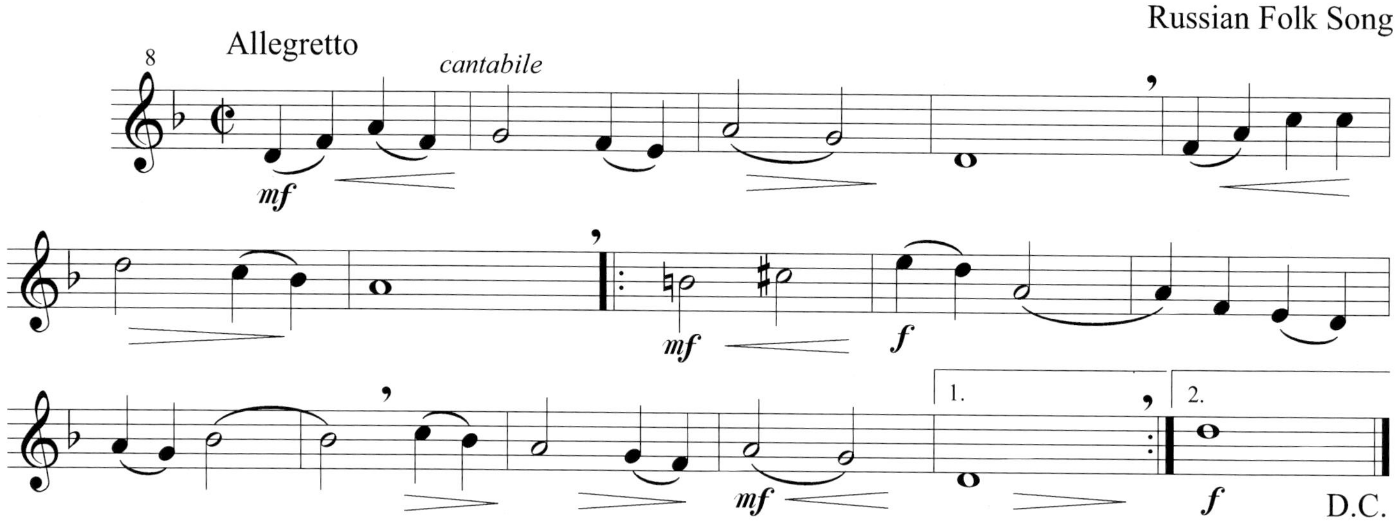

Children's Dance

Costel Puscoiu
(1951)

Krakowiak

Polish Folk Song

Pavane

Gabriel Fauré
(1845 - 1924)

Adagio

(from Clarinet Concerto)

Wolfgang Amadeus Mozart
(1756 - 1791)

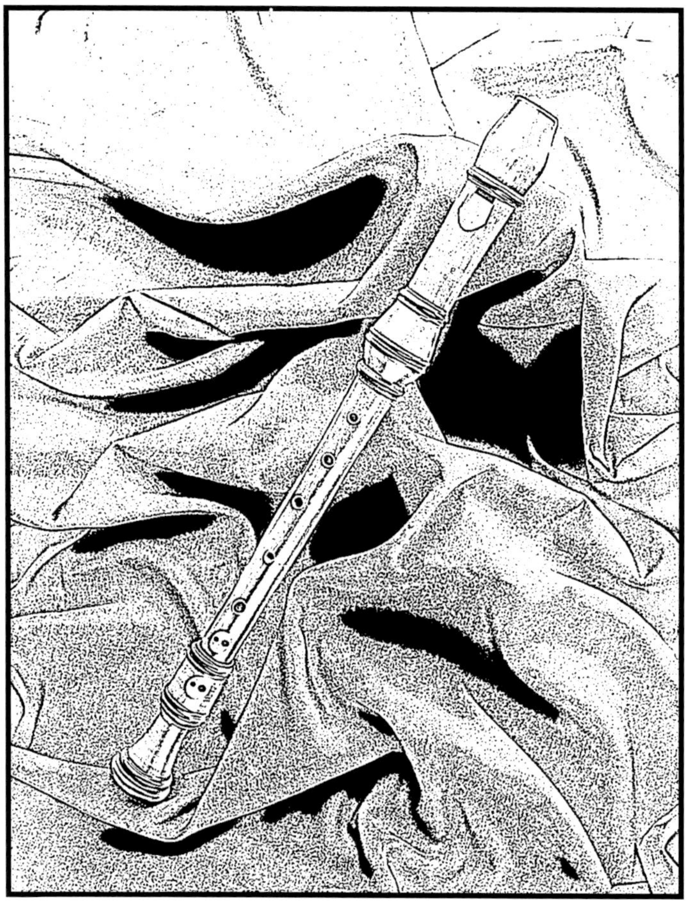

Prelude

(Op. 28, No. 7)

Frédéric Chopin
(1810-1849)

Two Pigeons

Argentinian Folk Song

Morning

(from "Peer Gynt")

Edvard Grieg
(1843 - 1907)

Album - leaf

(from "Lyric Pieces")

Edvard Grieg
(1843 - 1907)

Slavonic Dance

(Op. 46, No. 2)

Antonin Dvořák
(1841 - 1904)

Allegretto grazioso

Romance

(Op. 50)

Ludwig van Beethoven
(1770 - 1827)

Andante